ANCIENT MYTHOLOGY

POLYNESIAN MYTHS AND LEGENDS

by Alyssa Krekelberg
illustrated by Cesar Samaniego

Tools for Parents & Teachers

Grasshopper Books enhance imagination and introduce the earliest readers to fun storylines and illustrations. The easy-to-read text supports early reading experiences with repetitive sentence patterns and sight words.

Before Reading

- Discuss the cover illustration. What do readers see?
- Look at the glossary together. Discuss the words.

During Reading

- "Walk" through the book with the reader. Discuss new or unfamiliar words. Sound them out together.
- Look at the illustrations. When and where does the story take place? What is happening in the story?

After Reading

- Prompt the child to think more. Ask: What is your favorite Polynesian legend? Why?

Grasshopper Books are published by Jump!
3500 American Blvd W, Suite 150
Bloomington, MN 55431
www.jumplibrary.com

Copyright © 2026 Jump! International copyright reserved in all countries. No part of this book may be reproduced in any form without written permission from the publisher.

Jump! is a division of FlutterBee Education Group.

Library of Congress Cataloging-in-Publication Data

Names: Krekelberg, Alyssa, author.
Samaniego, César, 1975- illustrator.
Title: Polynesian myths and legends / by Alyssa Krekelberg; illustrated by Cesar Samaniego.
Description: Minneapolis, MN: Jump!, Inc. [2026]
Series: Ancient mythology | Includes index.
Audience: Ages 7-10 years
Identifiers: LCCN 2024052421 (print)
LCCN 2024052422 (ebook)
ISBN 9798892137621 (hardcover)
ISBN 9798892137638 (paperback)
ISBN 9798892137645 (ebook)
Subjects: LCSH: Legends–Polynesia–Juvenile literature.
Folklore–Polynesia–Juvenile literature.
Mythology, Polynesian–Juvenile literature.
Classification: LCC GR380 .K73 2026 (print)
LCC GR380 (ebook)
DDC 398.20996–dc23/eng/20241214
LC record available at https://lccn.loc.gov/2024052421
LC ebook record available at https://lccn.loc.gov/2024052422

Editor: Katie Chanez
Direction and Layout: Anna Peterson
Illustrator: Cesar Samaniego
Content Consultant: Dennis Kawaharada, PhD

Printed in the United States of America at Corporate Graphics in North Mankato, Minnesota.

Table of Contents

Legends from the Sea	4
Polynesian Gods and Goddesses	22
To Learn More	23
Glossary	24
Index	24

Legends from the Sea

At first, only water covered Earth. Tagaloa threw rocks into the Pacific Ocean. He made the first islands!

Tagaloa made a vine. When its leaves fell off, creatures came out. Tagaloa gave them heads, arms, legs, and hearts. They were the first humans!

The Pacific Ocean has many islands. Samoa, Hawai'i, New Zealand, Tonga, and Tahiti are some. This area is known as Polynesia.

Polynesian people have many different **cultures**. **Legends** of their gods and goddesses have been passed down for many years.

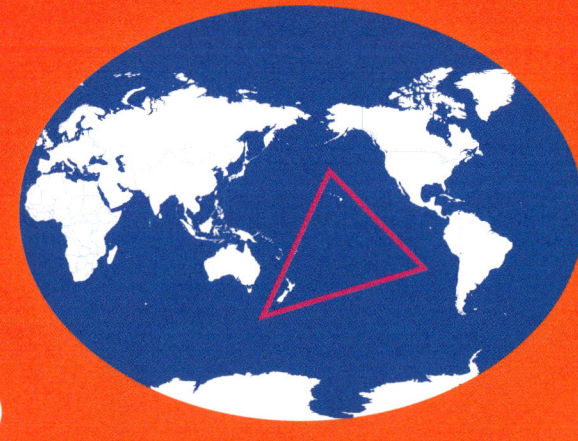

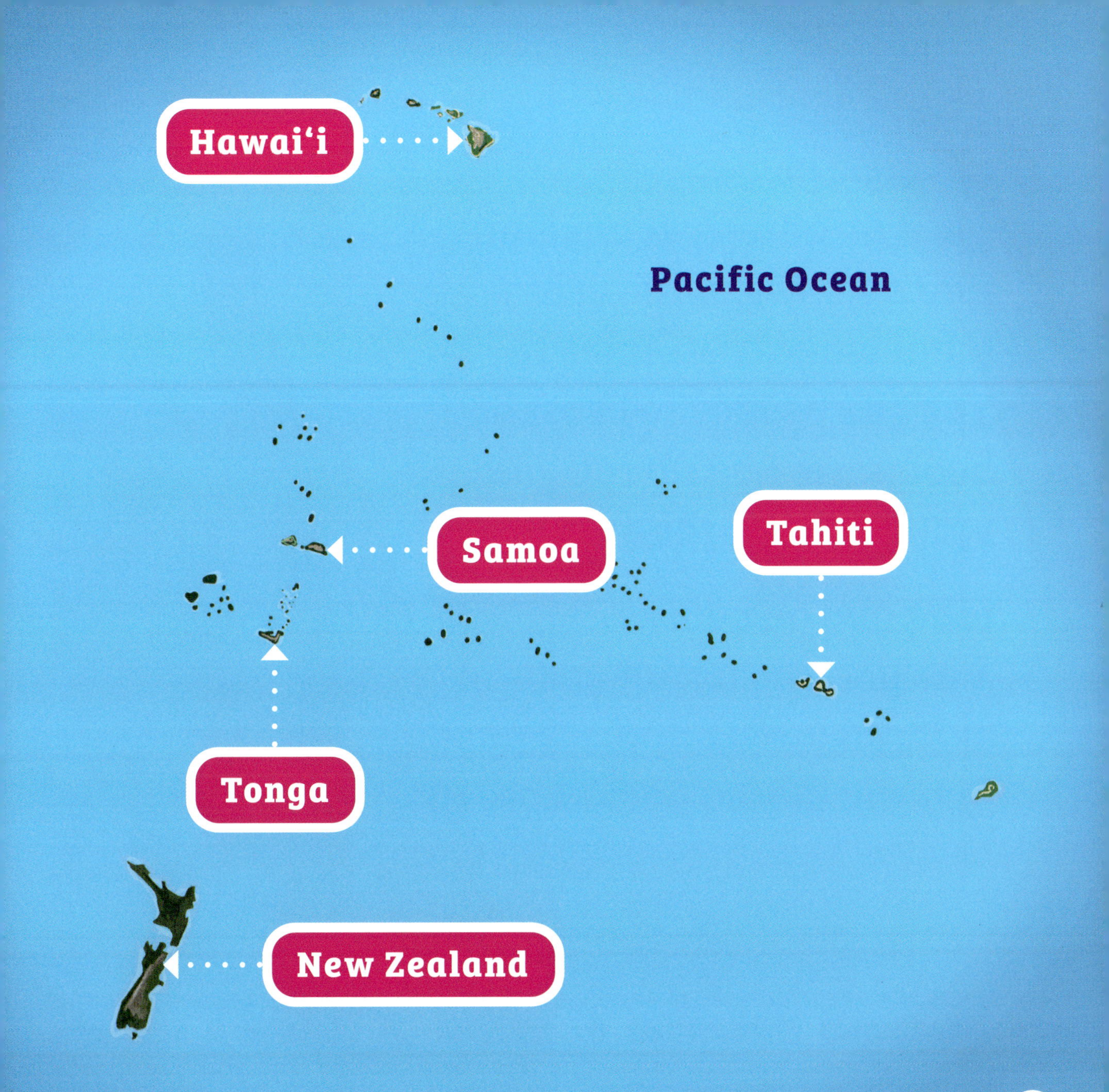
Hawai‘i
Pacific Ocean
Samoa
Tahiti
Tonga
New Zealand

The gods help people. On Tonga, an eel god fell in love with a princess. He told her to bury his head. The world's first coconut tree grew from the spot.

People drank the coconut water. They used the tree's wood to build homes. They used its leaves to make mats and baskets. The coconut tree made their lives easier.

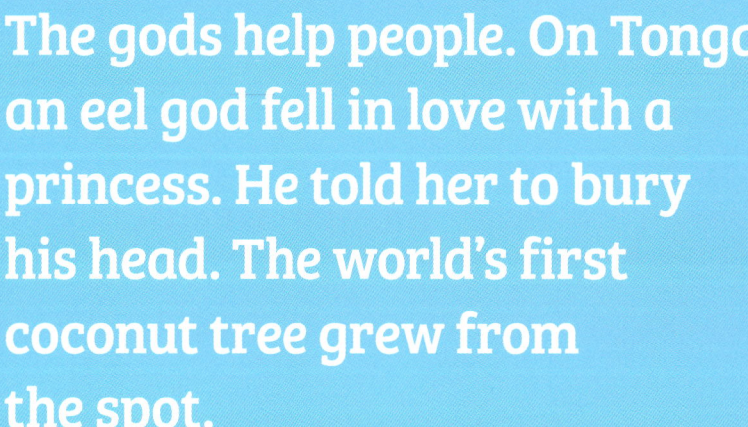

The Sun moved fast across the sky. Days were short. There was not much time to make food and do chores.

Maui is a **demigod**. He helps people. He tied up the Sun! The Sun begged to be let go. Maui made it promise to move slower in the sky. The Sun agreed. Maui made the days longer!

Only the fire goddess Mahuika could make fire. Maui wanted to change that. He tricked her. He put out her burning fingernails.

Mahuika was angry. She set the island on fire! Her fire was put into the trees. Maui told humans. They used wood to make fire for themselves!

Once, all fish looked the same. A **Māori** legend tells how that changed. Tangaroa, the god of the sea, was mad at humans. He ordered fish to scare them away.

As a reward, Tangaroa gave each fish what it asked for. The stingray got a long tail. The flounder got a flat body. Others got long, spear-like noses. Now, many different fish swim in the sea.

Hina was an adventurous woman. She left Tahiti with her brother. They sailed the ocean and visited many faraway islands.

Hina wanted to visit the Moon. She took her canoe there. She loved the Moon and decided to stay. She became the goddess of the Moon. At night, she watches over travelers on the sea.

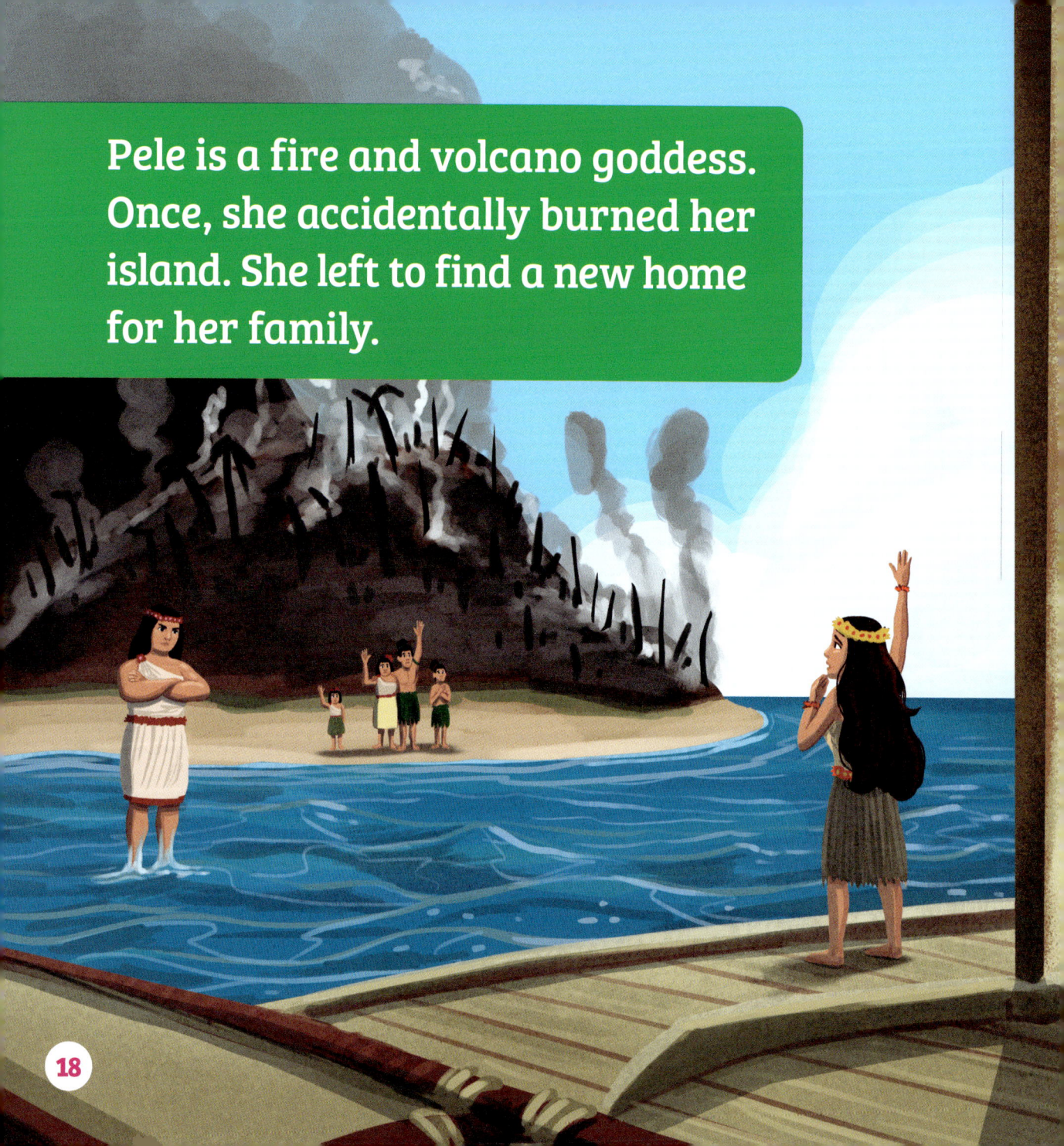

Pele is a fire and volcano goddess. Once, she accidentally burned her island. She left to find a new home for her family.

Pele reached Hawai'i. Her sister, Nā-maka-o-Kaha'i, was the goddess of the sea. She did not like Pele. She sent a wave of water.

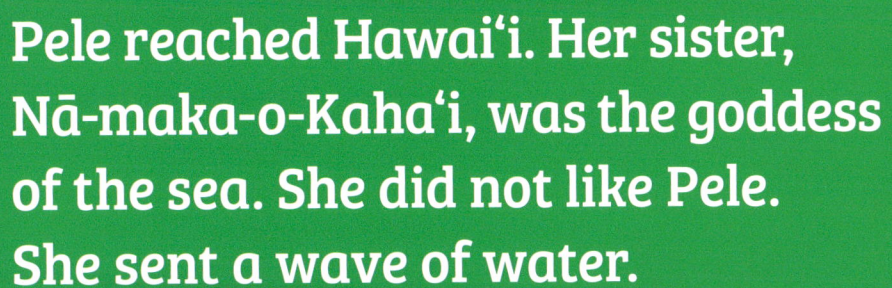

Nā-maka-o-Kaha'i

Pele and her sister fought. Pele's body was torn apart. But her **spirit** lived on. It flew to live in a volcano.

When Pele gets angry, the volcano **erupts**. When her lava enters the sea, it hardens and creates new land.

Polynesian Gods and Goddesses

Who are the most important Polynesian gods and goddesses? Take a look!

eel god
His head grew into the first coconut tree.

Hina
Tahitian goddess of the Moon

Mahuika
Māori fire goddess

Maui
Demigod and trickster

Nā-maka-o-Kahaʻi
Hawaiian goddess of the sea

Pele
Hawaiian fire and volcano goddess

Tagaloa
Samoan god of creation

Tangaroa
Māori god of the sea

To Learn More

Finding more information is as easy as 1, 2, 3.
❶ Go to www.factsurfer.com
❷ Enter "**Polynesianmythsandlegends**" into the search box.
❸ Choose your book to see a list of websites.

Glossary

cultures: The ideas, customs, traditions, and ways of life of groups of people.

demigod: Someone with more power than a human but less than a god.

erupts: Violently throws out lava, hot ashes, and steam.

legends: Stories handed down from earlier times.

Māori: Polynesian people native to New Zealand.

spirit: The part of a person that is believed to control thoughts and feelings.

Index

coconut tree 8

cultures 6

eel god 8

Hina 16

Mahuika 12, 13

Māori 14

Maui 10, 12, 13

Moon 16

Nā-maka-o-Kahaʻi 19, 20

Pacific Ocean 4, 6

Pele 18, 19, 20

Polynesia 6

Sun 10

Tagaloa 4, 5

Tangaroa 14

volcano 18, 20